Cursive Penmanship Workbook for Adults

Advanced Worksheets with a Modern Script Font and Inspiring Quotes for a Meaningful Practice

Not Your Typical Cursive Handwriting Workbook!

Cursive penmanship has become a lost artform. However, this workbook tries to revive that artform and combine the standard cursive style with modern calligraphy.

This book, therefore, was not designed to teach standard cursive handwriting, but something a bit more sophisticated. That's why it would be advantageous if you would already know how to write in the standard form of cursive. (If not, we have some great books designed to teach that too!)

So, what is this workbook really about? Essentially, it's an introduction to a handwriting style with calligraphic elements. This workbook builds upon the traditional handwriting style and allows you to discover an easy way of adding a nuanced touch of calligraphy to your handwriting.

It is designed for adults since it focuses on the cursive writing of entire sentences and paragraphs. Additionally, the font size is smaller compared to that of other standard children's practice worksheets.

This book contains a short practice section for each letter. It also includes recommendations on how each letter should be written. Each exercise revolves around a personal quote designed to inspire and motivate you. The quotes are simple and easy to understand, however, if applied in real life can have a big impact on you and the people around you.

At the beginning of each worksheet, you will find the quote written in a traceable cursive font. After retracing the entire quote, you should use the remaining space to rewrite the quote again.

In order to gain the most value out of this experience, you should not only practice the handwriting style presented here but also improve your knowledge by learning from the quotes included in this book. Read them carefully and let the true meaning of each sentence settle into your mind. We would recommend you take a moment after reading each quote and use it for reflection or even short meditations.

To offer a clear overview of the handwriting style presented in this workbook, we added a table with a comparison between the *Standard Cursive Style* and the *Modern Script Font* taught in this workbook.

Standard Cursive	Modern Script Font
A a	*A a*
B b	*B b*
C c	*C c*
D d	*D d*
E e	*E e*
F f	*F f*

G g	*G g*
H h	*H h*
I i	*I i*
J j	*J j*
K k	*K k*
L l	*L l*
M m	*M m*
N n	*N n*

$O\ o$	$O\ o$
$P\ p$	$P\ p$
$Q\ q$	$Q\ q$
$R\ r$	$R\ r$
$S\ s$	$S\ s$
$T\ t$	$T\ t$
$U\ u$	$U\ u$
$V\ v$	$V\ v$

W w	*W w*
X x	*X x*
Y y	*Y y*
Z z	*Z z*

Over time, you can allow this modern script font to evolve naturally and develop into something unique to your personality.

Tips for a Memorable Practice

This modern script font is a bit more difficult to master than the standard cursive style. That's why we also included some tips to get you started. These are not mandatory but could prove useful and turn the entire learning experience into something much more enjoyable:

1. Start with the right equipment

   As mentioned before, this style is a mix between standard handwriting and modern calligraphy. That's why any writing utensil could, in theory, be used. However, even if they are a bit tricky to master at first, pointed dib nips present obvious advantages when it comes to this style of writing. The pointed sharp nibs allow swirling flourishes and thin strokes to come much more easily.

2. Prepare the workspace

   First, you should clear the table and prepare a clean and organized practice environment.

   Second, you should prepare the supplies: a pen with a pointed dib nip (if you decided to use one), ink, the workbook, and additional paper.

3. Study each letter

   It might be tempting to go directly to the exercises and skip the individual letter practice. However, if you take a little bit of extra time to study and practice each letter, you will find it a lot easier to create a natural flow when writing entire words or sentences. You can even practice each letter on a blank paper to completely familiarize yourself with the motion.

4. Have fun

Remember that for such a style of handwriting to develop easily and evolve naturally, the entire practice must be enjoyed. The art of penmanship is something that can offer a unique touch to any written content. The learning experience should, therefore, be done with love so that the same feeling can be seen on paper.

A word of caution: During your practice, you might find it difficult to keep a steady flow during the hardwiring process. It's important to not get frustrated and keep practicing. This handwriting style depends entirely on steady strokes so don't get discouraged if the first few sentences won't be that "good-looking." Remember, over time you will develop a unique handwriting style filled with calligraphic elements which will embellish any written content of yours.

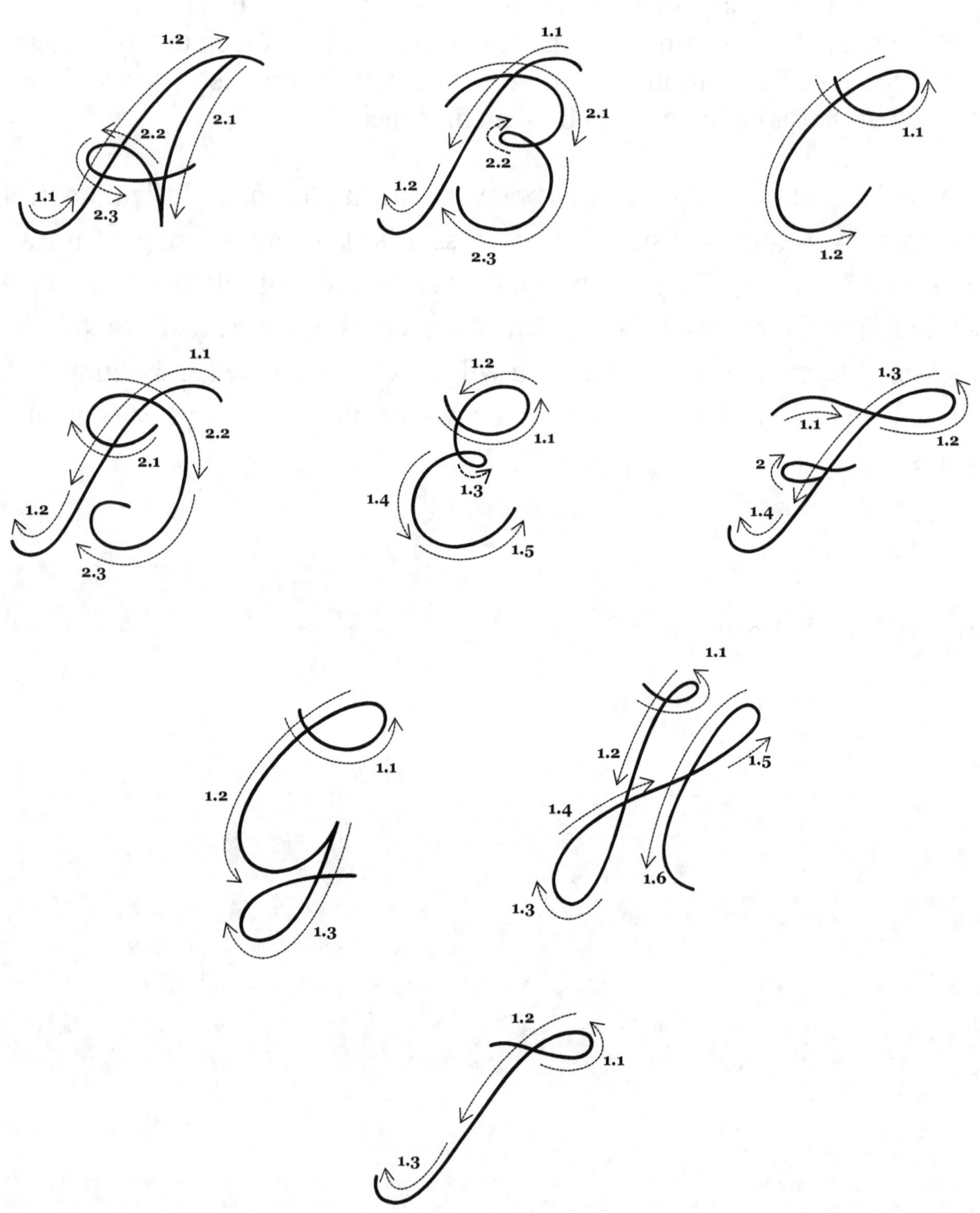

Modern script font - uppercase letters 2/3
(J, K, L, M, N, O, P, Q)

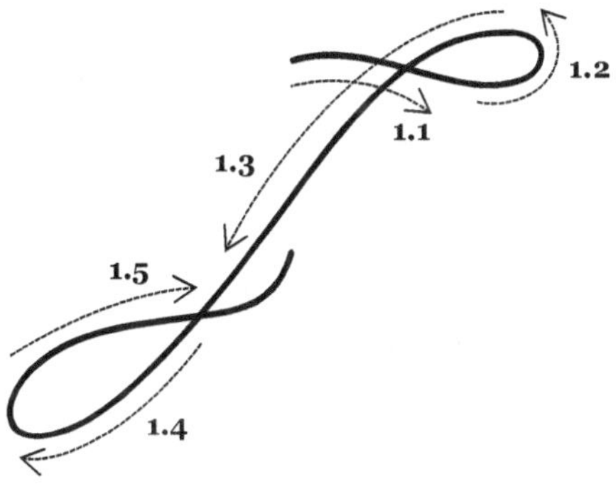

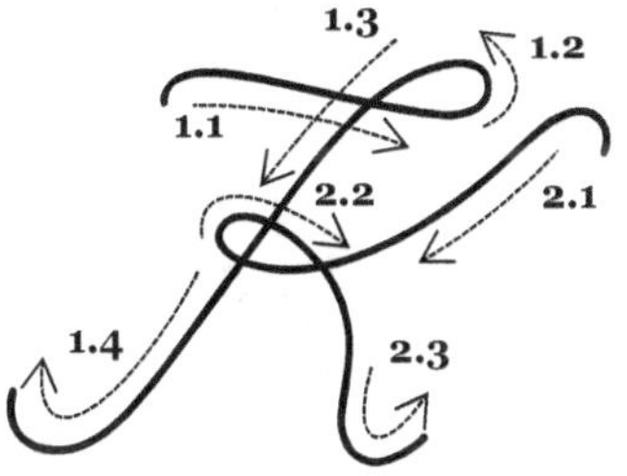

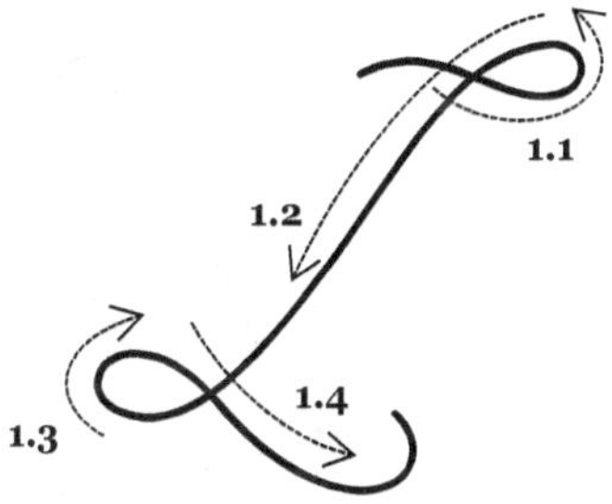

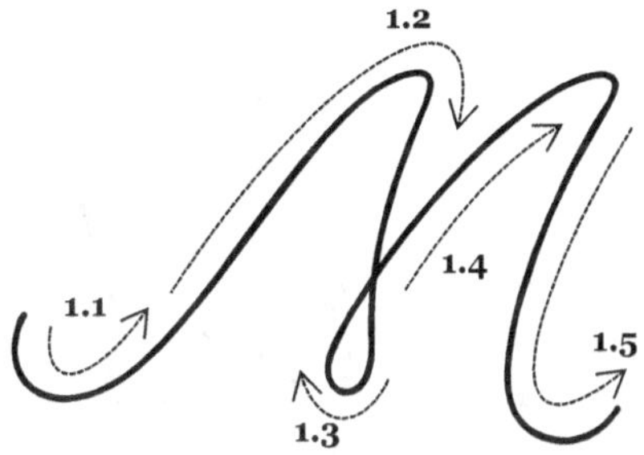

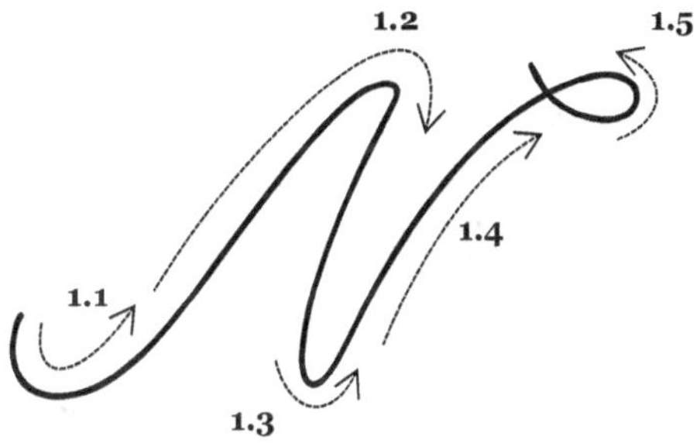

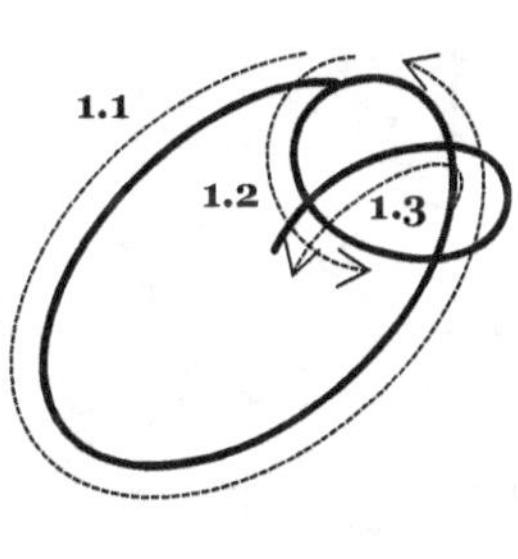

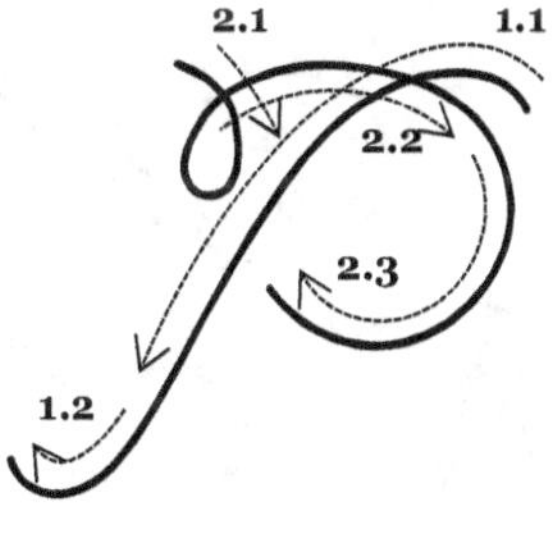

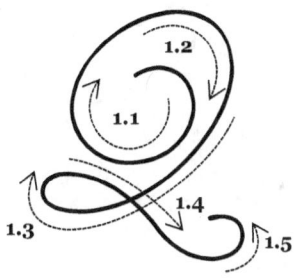

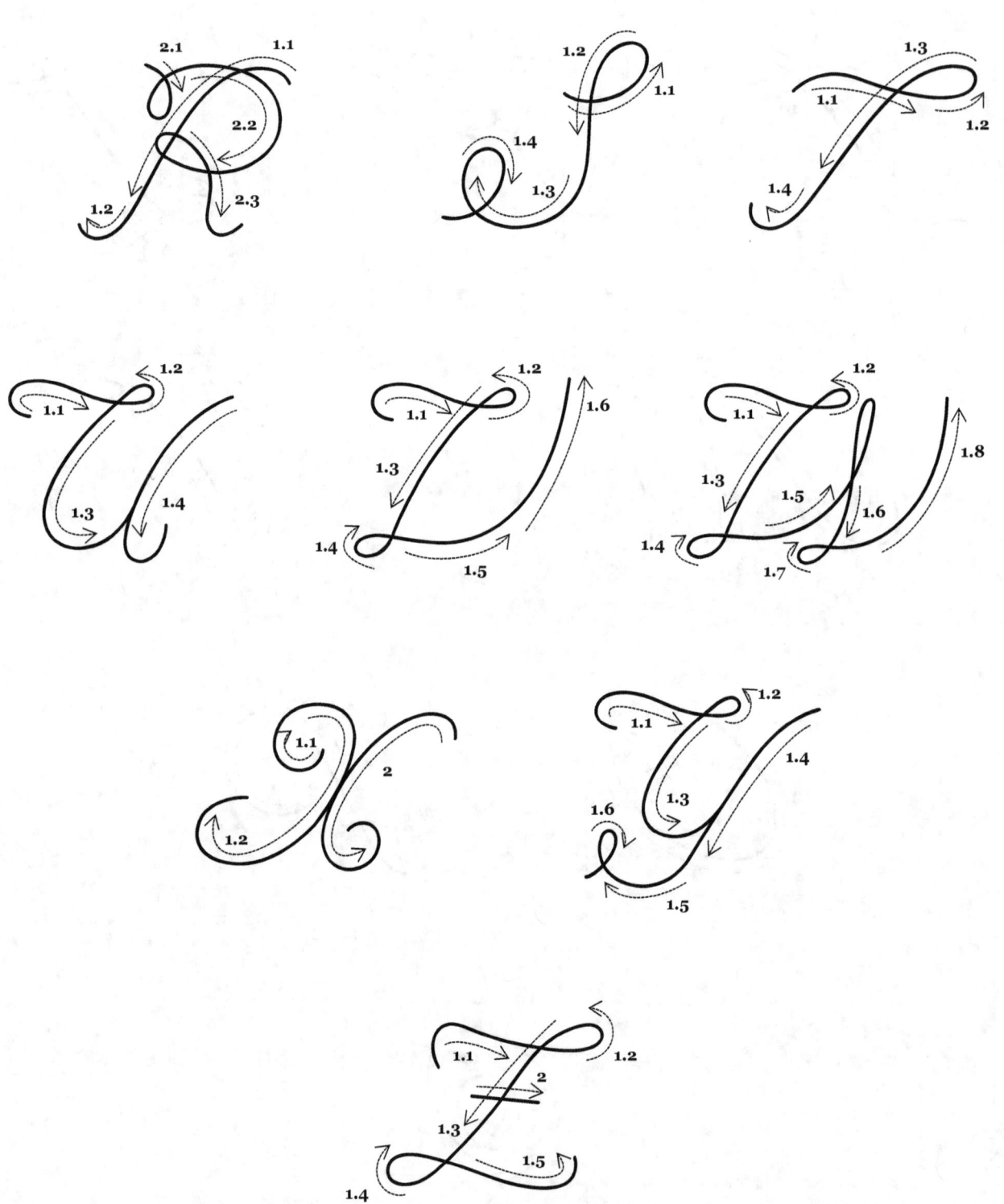

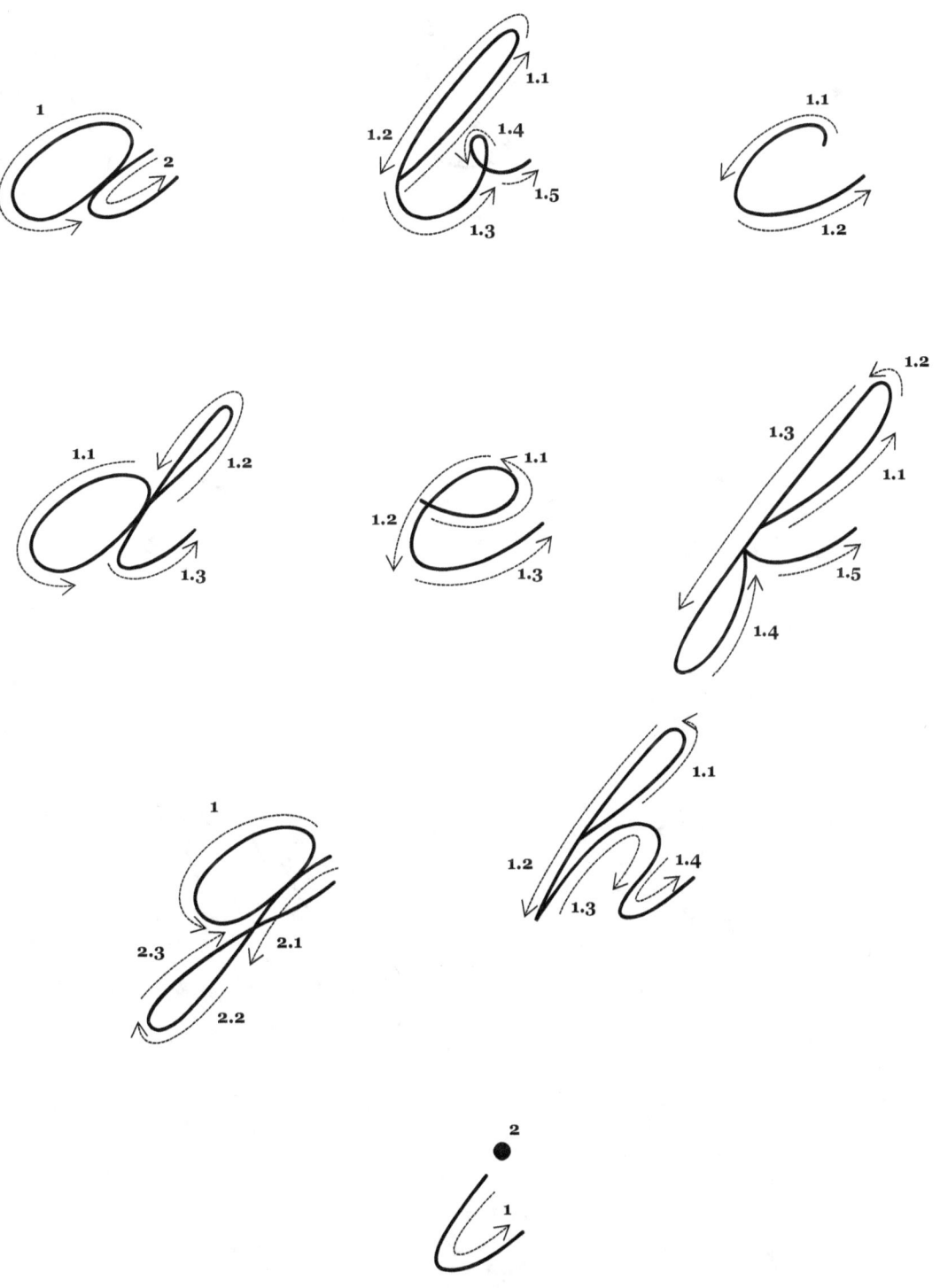

(j, k, l, m, n, o, p, q)

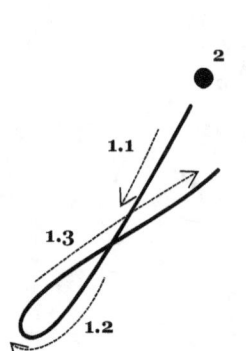

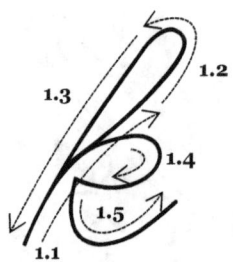

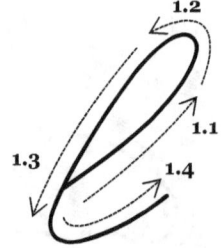

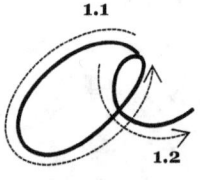

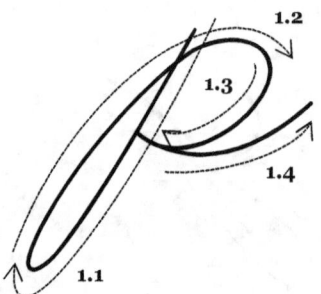

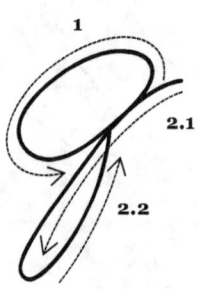

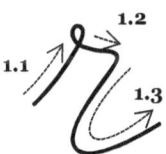
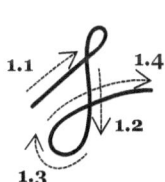
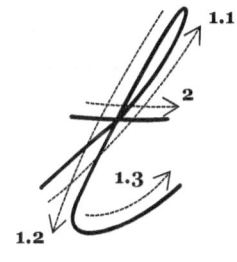

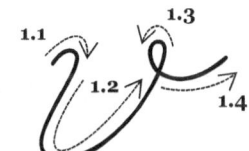
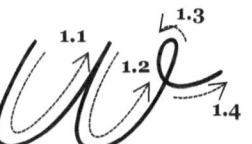

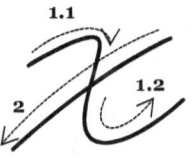
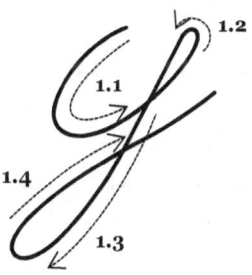

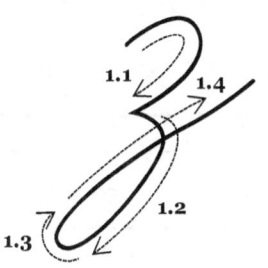

Modern script letter practice

A

a

B

b

C

c

D

d

E

e

F

f

G

g

H

h

I

i

J

j

K

k

L

l

M

m

N

n

O

Quote #1

Sometimes it's important to learn from the past.
Sometimes it's important to plan for the future. But
it's more important to learn to be happy in the here
and now.

Sometimes it's important
to learn from the past.
Sometimes it's important
to plan for the future.
But it's more important
to learn to be happy in
the here and now.

Quote #2

In order to inspire someone, you must first learn how to listen.

In order to inspire someone, you must first learn how to listen.

Every challenge is an opportunity to learn and grow.

Every challenge is an opportunity to learn and grow.

Don't let the failures of the past devour the
opportunities of the present.

Don't let the failures of
the past devour the
opportunities of the
present.

Quote #5

No matter how hard you try to avoid it,
failure is inevitable and that is a good thing. With
failure, there will always be knowledge.

No matter how hard you
try to avoid it, failure is
inevitable and that is a
good thing. With failure,
there will always be
knowledge.

Sometimes, what stops you from achieving your goals
are the limits you put on yourself.

Sometimes, what stops
you from achieving your
goals are the limits you
put on yourself.

No one is going to bring your dreams closer to you.
Only you can move towards them.

No one is going to bring
your dreams closer to
you. Only you can move
towards them.

Progress, no matter how small, is still progress.
Standing still is what keeps you from achieving it.

Progress, no matter how
small, is still progress.
Standing still is what
keeps you from achieving
it.

A decluttered environment leads to a decluttered mind.

A decluttered environment leads to a decluttered mind.

Don't expect others to solve your problems. Be your
own hero.

Don't expect others to
solve your problems. Be
your own hero.

The societal need for happiness should be the individual's need for happiness.

The societal need for

happiness should be the

individual's need for

happiness.

A weak person looks at others for advice at the first sign of trouble. Stop for a minute and think for yourself.

A weak person looks at others for advice at the first sign of trouble. Stop for a minute and think for yourself.

Quote #13

When you feel like you have reached your limit, don't
be afraid to ask for help.

When you feel like you
have reached your limit,
don't be afraid to ask for
help.

<u>Quote #14</u>

Always take responsibility for your actions, even if you've made a mistake. Being responsible offers you control and allows you to learn and evolve.

Always take responsibility

for your actions, even if

you've made a mistake.

Being responsible offers

you control and allows

you to learn and evolve.

A wise man always knows that there is something new to learn.

A wise man always knows that there is something new to learn.

If you expect to be respected by everyone, then be
respectful to everyone.

If you expect to be
respected by everyone,
then be respectful to
everyone.

You can always choose to do something good. Be
grateful. Be kind. Be happy.

You can always choose to
do something good. Be
grateful. Be kind. Be
happy.

Greatness in life cannot be achieved without sacrifice.

Greatness in life cannot be

achieved without sacrifice.

Commitment comes with success: you just have to be
willing to endure and be patient.

Commitment comes with
success: you just have to
be willing to endure and
be patient.

We either stress about the past or worry about the future, but we tend to forget that history is being made right here and now.

We either stress about the
past or worry about the
future, but we tend to
forget that history is
being made right here
and now.

When we start lying to others, we begin by lying to
ourselves.

When we start lying to
others, we begin by lying
to ourselves.

Learn to keep your word. Integrity will conquer any
excuse your mind can come up with.

Learn to keep your word.

Integrity will conquer

any excuse your mind can

come up with.

Most people say that a schedule robs you of your
freedom and then they spend the entire day
deciding what to do.

Most people say that a
schedule robs you of your
freedom and then they
spend the entire day
deciding what to do.

Knowledge is a tool that can turn an idea into reality.

Knowledge is a tool that can turn an idea into reality.

Opportunities are everywhere, but most of us are too
afraid to acknowledge them.

Opportunities are
everywhere, but most of
us are too afraid to
acknowledge them.

Instant gratification can also lead to instant
suffering.

Instant gratification can
also lead to instant
suffering.

Living a lie will always end in disappointment. The sooner we accept that, the sooner we can begin to set ourselves free and be wary, for the road to freedom is a difficult one.

Living a lie will always
end in disappointment.
The sooner we accept
that, the sooner we can
begin to set ourselves free
and be wary, for the road
to freedom is a difficult
one.

If you turn your back on a problem, it doesn't make it disappear.

If you turn your back on a problem, it doesn't make it disappear.

You can choose to be brave, you can choose to be kind, you can choose to be committed. You can always choose.

You can choose to be
brave, you can choose to
be kind, you can choose to
be committed. You can
always choose.

The greatest tool you have at your disposal is your mind. Cherish it. train it. use it.

The greatest tool you
have at your disposal is
your mind. Cherish it.
train it. use it.

Laziness will never lead to greatness.

Laziness will never lead to greatness.

In order to stop feeling lonely, you first need to learn how to be alone.

In order to stop feeling
lonely, you first need to
learn how to be alone.

The only way to conquer your fears is to find the
courage to face them.

The only way to conquer
your fears is to find the
courage to face them.

Find something you love doing and you will excel at
it with ease.

Find something you love
doing and you will excel
at it with ease.

Sometimes, the best answer lies right in front of us.
We just like to overlook it.

Sometimes, the best
answer lies right in front
of us. We just like to
overlook it.

One of the greatest powers someone can have is to learn how to be comfortable with themselves.

One of the greatest
powers someone can have
is to learn how to be
comfortable with
themselves.

If you are able to do something good in this world.
then you are also responsible for doing it.

If you are able to do
something good in this
world. then you are also
responsible for doing it.

First find the courage to be yourself. Then commit yourself to becoming the best version of that self.

First find the courage to be yourself. Then commit yourself to becoming the best version of that self.

Stop dreaming about doing great things and start
doing them!

Stop dreaming about
doing great things and
start doing them!

Do not be afraid of your dreams.

Do not be afraid of your
dreams.

<u>Quote #41</u>

Even if you don't know how to reach your dreams,
start moving towards them – the right path will
become clear as you go.

Even if you don't know
how to reach your
dreams, start moving
towards them – the right
path will become clear
as you go.

All you need is the courage to take one more step. As long as you continue, you will reach your goals eventually.

All you need is the courage to take one more step. As long as you continue, you will reach your goals eventually.

Don't stay wondering whether something is right for
you or not. Take action and give it a go.

Don't stay wondering
whether something is
right for you or not.
Take action and give
it a go.

Most of us start fearing death before we even start living.

Most of us start fearing
death before we even
start living.

There is only one way to overcome procrastination.
Begin now!

There is only one way to
overcome procrastination.
Begin now!

Do not expect a grand gesture that will change your
life or you will die expecting.

Do not expect a grand

gesture that will change

your life or you will die

expecting.

You will never feel 100% ready. So why not start today?

You will never feel 100% ready. So why not start today?

When you diverge away from the beaten track you
start laying out a path for others to follow.

When you diverge away
from the beaten track
you start laying out a
path for others to
follow.

Some of the greatest lessons in life are preceded by risk.

Some of the greatest
lessons in life are
preceded by risk.

Quote #50

At some point, you need to stop reading about the adventures of others and start writing about your own.

At some point, you need to stop reading about the adventures of others and start writing about your own.

Don't copy something old. Create something new.

Don't copy something old.
Create something new.

Dare to aim high and jump towards the sky.

Dare to aim high and
jump towards the sky.

You can rest by moving forward a bit slower.

You can rest by moving forward a bit slower.

Quote #54

Never wait for your dreams to come closer. Move towards them as fast as you can.

Never wait for your

dreams to come closer.

Move towards them as

fast as you can.

Quote #55

If you want to achieve something, it should not be to impress others, but to impress yourself.

If you want to achieve
something, it should not
be to impress others, but
to impress yourself.

Do not expect to achieve your long-term dreams
without sacrificing some short-term pleasures.

Do not expect to achieve
your long-term dreams
without sacrificing some
short-term pleasures.

A challenge is always accompanied by an opportunity. You just have to stay calm and recognize it.

A challenge is always
accompanied by an
opportunity. You just
have to stay calm and
recognize it.

<u>Quote #58</u>
Whatever you try to do,
do it in the best way you can.

Whatever you try to do,
do it in the best way you
can.

No dream will wait for someone to wake up.

No dream will wait for

someone to wake up.

A true friend is someone who supports your dreams.
even if he doesn't share them.

A true friend is someone
who supports your dreams.
even if he doesn't share
them.

Quote #61

A single good idea has the power to change the world.

A single good idea has

the power to change the

world.

Books are great: knowledge and preparation are essential for success. But nothing will ever trump experience.

Books are great: know-
ledge and preparation
are essential for success.
But nothing will ever
trump experience.

Our fears are only as strong as we allow them to be.

Our fears are only as strong as we allow them to be.

A life free from fear is a life of true liberty.

*A life free from fear is a
life of true liberty.*

When you feel overrun with fear, take a second,
acknowledge it, and then do what scares you anyway.

When you feel overrun
with fear, take a second,
acknowledge it, and then
do what scares you
anyway.

The greatest enemy of the human mind is fear.

The greatest enemy of the human mind is fear.

Worry is the destroyer of all productivity.

Worry is the destroyer of
all productivity.

Never let temptations break your principles.

Never let temptations
break your principles.

Sometimes being silent is the best course of action.

Sometimes being silent is
the best course of action.

Quote #70

Never do something you don't want to do just to impress others.

Never do something you
don't want to do just to
impress others.

Always keep an open mind. Knowledge can be
improved at all ages.

Always keep an open

mind. Knowledge can be

improved at all ages.

No matter what generation we live in, being humble and grateful for one's blessings will never go out of style.

No matter what gene-
nation we live in, being
humble and grateful for
one's blessings will never
go out of style.

Quote #73

People often ask for more than they actually need
because they never stop to think about what they
actually want.

People often ask for more
than they actually need
because they never stop
to think about what they
actually want.

Personal development starts with personal
acknowledgment.

Personal development
starts with personal
acknowledgment.

Quote #75

Most of our problems only exist in our minds.
We like to overcomplicate things and imagine
trouble when there isn't any.

Most of our problems
only exist in our minds.
We like to overcompli-
cate things and imagine
trouble when there isn't
any.

Quote #76

Virtues are habits: you aren't born with them, you practice them.

Virtues are habits: you aren't born with them, you practice them.

Trusting your heart is just as important as trusting your mind.

Trusting your heart is just as important as trusting your mind.

If you are not looking for an answer, it will remain
hidden forever...maybe even in plain sight.

If you are not looking for
an answer, it will remain
hidden forever...maybe
even in plain sight.

Quote #79

The most substantial growth happens outside of your comfort zone.

The most substantial growth happens outside of your comfort zone.

Anger will never offer good advice.

Anger will never offer

good advice.

Anger will never offer good advice.

The greater the success,
the greater the dangers.
Don't fear them but be
aware of them.

Never tell anyone how great you are – show them.

Never tell anyone how great you are – show them.

Quote #83

*Don't expect anything from life
that you did not earn.*

*Don't expect anything
from life that you did
not earn.*

Never let negative words break you. If they are true, learn from them. If they are false, ignore them.

Never let negative words
break you. If they are
true, learn from them. If
they are false, ignore
them.

If you are always truthful to the world, you will always be truthful to yourself.

If you are always
truthful to the world, you
will always be truthful to
yourself.

www.ingramcontent.com/pod-product-compliance
Lightning Source LLC
Chambersburg PA
CBHW081400280526
45788CB00009B/2937